French Chic. The Ultimate Guide to French Fashion, Beauty and Style

Dress Classy and Elegant on Any Budget

Forward your Amazon purchase receipt to **foreverchiclife@gmail.com in order to receive your FREE printable French Chic Daily Affirmations Poster.**

Table of Contents

Introduction

Chapter 1 - French Style & Beauty – An Introduction

Chapter 2 - The Art of Dressing Elegantly

Chapter 3 - How to Build Your Signature Look

Chapter 4 - What Not to Wear

Chapter 5 - Hair, Grooming and Make-Up

Chapter 6 - The Basics of Chic – Inner Values

Chapter 7 - Shopping Tips for the Elegant Woman

Conclusion

© **Copyright 2016 by Veronique Antoinette Blanchard - All Rights Reserved.**

This book is geared towards providing exact and reliable information with regards to the topic and issue covered. The publication is sold with the idea that the publisher is not required to render accounting, officially permitted, or otherwise, qualified services. If advice is necessary, legal or professional, a practiced individual in the profession should be ordered.

- From a Declaration of Principles which was accepted and approved equally by a Committee of the American Bar Association and a Committee of Publishers and Associations.

In no way is it legal to reproduce, duplicate, or transmit any part of this document in either electronic means or in printed format. Recording of this publication is strictly prohibited and any storage of this document is not allowed unless with written permission from the publisher. All rights reserved.

The information provided herein is stated to be truthful and consistent, in that any liability, in terms of inattention or otherwise, by any usage or abuse of any policies, processes, or directions contained within is the solitary and utter responsibility of the recipient reader. Under no circumstances will any legal responsibility or blame be held against the publisher for any reparation, damages, or monetary loss due to the information herein, either directly or indirectly.

Respective authors own all copyrights not held by the publisher.

The information herein is offered for informational purposes solely and is universal as so. The presentation of the information is without a contract or any type of guaranteed assurance.

The trademarks that are used are without any consent, and the publication of the trademark is without permission or backing by the trademark owner. All trademarks and brands within this book are for clarifying purposes only and are the owned by the owners themselves, not affiliated with this document.

Introduction

I want to thank you and congratulate you for investing in this book. I have done my best to provide value to you and I really hope that you will enjoy reading this book. This book contains proven steps and strategies on how to dress classy and elegant like a French woman on any budget. You can trust the information presented in this book as it comes from a native Parisian.

Having been born in this iconic city, world famous for its romantic charm and fashionable women, I grew up watching an impeccably dressed mother. Her personal style inspired my own as the art of being beautifully dressed came naturally and rather effortlessly to her. While I had heard about how French style is admired all over the world, I realized just how different the French way of life is only during my stay in the US.

I moved to the US for work. I was working as a fashion buyer for a major fashion house. During my 6 year stay there, I had ample opportunity to understand the differences between the dressing style of French women and that of American women. While my American friends admired my personal sense of style, my less is more philosophy (which is innately French) was a source of major fascination to them. Later on, when I moved back to Paris, one of my American friends visited me here. She was totally amazed by the tiny closet space found pretty much everywhere in Europe. I am writing this book to resolve the mystery behind how French women manage to look so chic while fitting all their possessions into a comparatively small wardrobe.

French women whose style I truly admire include Brigitte Bardot, Carla Bruni and Jane Birkin. However, my greatest fashion icon of all time has always been Jackie Kennedy (despite the fact that she was American, she truly represented the iconic French style). Women like her possess a timeless appeal and their sense of style is relevant to every era. Since childhood I have known that this was how I wanted to be. Therefore, I spent years evolving my personal style around a timeless and classic look.

Classic French style is essentially based on simplicity and elegance. We'll discuss the wardrobe must haves essential for this kind of look but you must modify those basics to match your own true style.

This will require being observant of your personal likes and dislikes. You'll have to pay attention to what truly appeals to you and what complements your body structure.

I developed my own style by observing the minutest details that appeal to me. For instance, I noticed that the only kind of prints that truly appeal to me involves small floral ones. This matches my personal ultra-feminine romantic style.

The better you understand yourself, the better you'll know your style. The magic of wearing clothes that truly complement your personality is that it enhances your entire being in a subtle but incredibly profound way.

While this book will empower you with the knowledge you need to look super chic day in and day out, knowing and developing your own personal style will help you add a personal signature to every look you create.

Now, without further ado, let's get started with the basics of building a French chic wardrobe or rather an entire way of life.

Thanks again for downloading this book, I hope you enjoy it!

Chapter 1 - French Style & Beauty – An Introduction

It is said that Parisians live in shoebox-sized apartments. Yet despite the limited closet space, they seem to harbor the secret to effortless chic. What makes French fashion so legendary is the fact that it looks so effortless while still being a class apart. If there is one word that can be used to define French fashion, then it has to be 'simplicity.'

The Psychology of Excess and The French Philosophy of Minimalism

In America, the philosophy seems to be the bigger, the better – and this applies to people's closets as well. Fast fashion makes it super easy to buy and discard clothes at alarming speed. Most of my American friends complain about not having anything to wear in their gigantic wardrobes. Clothes that are bought as last minute deals are either worn once or twice or they just continue sitting in one's closet with tags intact never seeing the light of day.

In France, we usually focus on buying less while investing in high-quality pieces at the same time. My personal philosophy has always been to possess a few basic items that can easily be mixed and matched to create any look. I have always ensured that these staples should be of the highest possible quality which certainly also implies that they are expensive. However, the true value of a garment is not merely determined by the sticker price one pays initially but by the amount of wear one gets out of it.

If I am buying a cheap dress on sale which I was to wear only once, this would amount to sheer extravagance. Whereas, my black silk skirt which came at a very high sticker price is a wardrobe staple I have been wearing for years. It's something that never goes out of style and the amount of wear I have gotten out of it, completely compensates for the initial cost I incurred in purchasing it.

What's the French Secret

The reason why French style is universally loved is because of the fact that it is timeless and simple. The elegance that a French woman carries comes from a sense of effortless simplicity. Despite the effort that goes into keeping such an attractive appearance, the entire look appears effortlessly chic. If you truly aspire to dress like a French woman, then you must embrace simplicity. An elegant woman is, after all, a lady of simple but highly refined taste.

She does not follow fashion fads and passing trends. Her wardrobe comprises timeless classics that can be easily mixed and matched to create any look. If you want to dress like an elegant French woman, then you will have to adopt the mindset of long-term thinking. Your shopping habits will no longer center around finding the best discounts but around finding pieces you can derive maximum value out of.

Thinking Like a French Woman

Always opt for the highest quality pieces you can afford. If you start planning your wardrobe with a long-term vision, then you'll realize how the clothes you bought super cheap are actually more extravagant purchases than some of your truly expensive outfits. How? Think about this: if you wore an item of clothing only once, then what is its true cost in the long-run? On the contrary, if you bought a high-quality expensive outfit that you ended up wearing many times, isn't it cheaper in the long run. Plus, you can't discount the fact that it adds to your self-confidence and happiness!

Splurge on Essentials

Instead of window shopping for the latest trends, evaluate your list of essentials. Well-cut pants, silk blouses in solid colors, a well-tailored skirt suit, a jacket in a timeless design are all essentials (we will throw greater light on wardrobe staples in another chapter). The key here is to acquire all pieces in colors that can be easily mixed and match. Trendy clothes never last the test of time but a wardrobe built on the foundation of essentials is there to stay for years and maybe even a decade or two. Never skimp when shopping for essentials. Remember that this is a long-term investment which will eventually save you money.

Choose Your fabrics with Care

Stick to natural fabrics as much as you can. Synthetic fabrics are not only uncomfortable to wear but are also often less sturdy. Besides, the look and feel of high-quality natural fabrics is way superior to what the best quality synthetics can ever provide. Indeed, there are some man-made fabrics that almost completely resemble naturals, it is still best to steer clear of them. At the most, you can opt for blends but something like a hundred percent polyester dress is best avoided at all costs.

Therefore, while shopping, do not just take into account the design and cut of the outfit but also how you'll feel inside it. Think about how your skin will feel next to the fabric, how comfortable you'll be in it, and only then go ahead to make a purchase.

Cut and Craftsmanship

How an outfit is cut and sewn together can totally make or break the look. Even the most expensive fabric can look cheap if the design and cut of the outfit do not boast of excellent craftsmanship. Again, add only quality pieces to your wardrobe and calculate the value of your clothes not in term of their label price but in terms of how many times you'll wear them, how it will make you feel and the compliments they will bring to you.

Exercise - Closet Detox

Think about how many times you have stood in front of your closet mourning the fact that you have nothing to wear. You must understand that this is what happens when you rely on impulse rather than on planning when you go shopping.

I would suggest doing a wardrobe cleanse before moving any further with this book. Plan a day when you would take the time to go through every item in your closet. Try out every item you wish to keep and add to your charity stack whatever you wish to give away.

Now, it is easy to get carried away with wanting to keep that one, two, three or maybe innumerable pieces of clothing which you think you'll want to wear someday even if you have no desire them anytime soon.

This is why it is smarter to do this exercise with someone you trust. In moments of weakness, your partner will help you in retaining focus on your goal. Remember the ultimate goal of this exercise is to get rid of everything that you haven't worn in a year and will likely never wear again. You must also get rid of clothes that no longer fit you. Yes, you do have the choice of getting them tailored to fit you better but sometimes letting them go might be a better choice.

The amazing thing about this exercise is that you will suddenly feel lighter as if a weight has been lifted off your shoulders. Being surrounded only by the clothes you will give you a lot of joy every time you look at your closet.

Chapter 2 – The Art of Dressing Elegantly

Dressing elegantly is an art – it's all about looking effortlessly classy and presentable. If you want to dress elegantly, then you must embrace simplicity and steer clear of following trends. I personally have a four-pronged approach to dressing elegantly. I call it the CFDA rule. CFDA stands for Color, Fit, Design, and Accessorizing. Let's discuss each one of these in detail now.

The Magic of Colors

To any discerning pair of eyes, it is more than obvious that certain colors look more elegant than others. On the streets of Paris, one color that seems to be universally popular is black. Indeed, black is certainly one of the chicest colors within the color spectrum. The reason why black is so popular is because it exudes a sense of timeless elegance while giving one a very flattering silhouette.

In my personal opinion, the colors that are absolutely essential to an elegant wardrobe are black, navy, wine, white and red. These colors are almost universally flattering to any woman and can really make any outfit stand out. You can experiment with different hues and shades of these colors.

Of course, pastel shades are also essential for an elegant wardrobe, especially during summertime. Pastel shades are also usually universally flattering. You can pick a few of your favorite shades and stick to them.

If you want to look classic and chic, then you really don't want to experiment too much with color. Stick to the ones you know suit you best.

Colors you definitely want to stay away from include: yellow, orange, fluorescent. These are truly risqué colors that more often than not, look unflattering. This is more a suggestion than an injunction. If you absolutely feel that a particular shade of any of these colors looks good on you, then, by all means, you can go ahead and experiment with it. However, if you have the slightest doubt about it, then staying off it will be the smartest choice.

Define The Colors That Suit You Best

It is much smarter and also a lot more cost-effective to build an entire wardrobe based on a relatively narrow spectrum of colors that suit you best. This way every time you buy a new piece, you'll get it in a color that goes with the rest of your wardrobe. Every time you are tempted to buy a new item, you must assess whether it will go with your current wardrobe or not because the true cost of the outfit isn't determined only by the sticker price you pay for it but by how much you have to pay to create an entire look using it. If you already have items that match your new purchase, it significantly reduces the total cost.

Follow these guidelines to make the color selections for your wardrobe:

Top/Dresses

4-6 colors - (I'll definitely recommend adding black as a staple here. Even if it looks too harsh against your skin, you can always soften the look by adding a pearl necklace or a lovely scarf. Another color which is almost universally flattering and timelessly elegant is navy blue. I would, therefore, highly recommend adding it to your list).

Trousers/Bottoms/Skirts/Jeans

2-3 colors - (I would recommend owning at least one pair in Black and another one in white).

Accessories (Bags/shoes/wallet)

I would recommend owning an entire set of accessories in tan and another one in black. If you can't invest in both the colors at the moment, then start out with tan first as it has the ability to go with just about any color including black and white.

Other accessories (Scarves/jackets)

You can get really playful when selecting scarves and jackets. Choose bright and vibrant colors for adding interest to any outfit. I would highly recommend owning jackets in bright red, blue and white. Again, be sure to choose your scarves and jackets in the highest quality fabrics. Stick to silk, wool and pashmina when selecting your scarves. They add an elegant luxurious look to any outfit. Similarly, with jackets, choose the highest quality natural fabrics you can afford.

Prints and Patterns

It is best to stay away from prints and patterns as much as possible since these can often be difficult to carry. You don't have to give up on prints entirely – just make sure that you are more careful when choosing them. Smaller prints often tend to look more elegant.

Solid colors provide several advantages. First of all, they give you a more svelte appearance. Secondly, when you wear just one color from shoulder to hem, it creates a long vertical line making you appear tall and lean.

When it comes to patterns, opt for vertical lines as they'll make you appear taller. Horizontal lines, on the other hand, lead the eyes from side-to-side making one appear heavier and broader. It is best to not let horizontal lines be a dominant pattern in any outfit.

Diagonal lines can also have a lengthening effect as long as they fall vertically for the most part. Opt for diagonal lines that form a V shape as this will have a slimming effect on your silhouette. The body will appear slimmest at the point where the diagonal lines form a V. At the same time, the body will appear wider at the point where the V diverges.

Curved lines are excellent for enhancing the curves. Opt for curve-enhancing patterns whenever you can as they look elegant and gloriously feminine.

Necklines

One of the most prominent features of a dress is its neckline – it can completely make or break a look. Very often it is also the most visible element of an outfit as the neckline is what remains visible even when you are sitting at your office desk or a restaurant.

V necklines are amongst the most elegant. However, they look truly chic only when they are exaggeratedly low-cut almost down to the waist. They make the neck appear longer and slimmer. You can also create this kind of effect by wearing a string of long chains (not too bulky). Similarly, this effect can be created by leaving an oblong scarf hanging loose or by knotting it quite low.

While this kind of neckline looks classy on nearly all body types, they are especially highly recommended for women with short necks. Such women should also stay away from necklines that fall directly on the neck like jewel neck or high-collar button-down styles. It is also best for them to stay away from turtlenecks.

Women with long necks can get more adventurous with necklines. One very flattering style is the boat neck which can look very elegant and sophisticated.

Décolleté necklines worn in the evening also look extremely alluring and dramatic. They can be worn by women with shorter necks also. However, a truly classy woman would wear a décolleté neckline only on a formal evening out. They are just too risqué for daytime and can reflect poor taste when worn in the wrong surroundings.

It is best to steer clear of unflattering styles like the scoop neck or the U neck that look quite unbecoming on nearly all kinds of women. Asymmetrical necklines can also be tricky to wear and should be avoided at all cost unless they are part of an evening dress draped in the Grecian style. That's pretty much the only time an asymmetrical neckline looks truly elegant.

Another type of neckline which can look quite flattering on nearly all types of necks is the cowl neckline. The softly draped look this neckline creates is flattering on all women.

Hems

While hemlines can go up or down depending upon the wearer's taste, an elegant woman would ideally try to stay away from hemlines that are too high. Longer hemlines are also a lot more figure flattering and make one appear taller. Of course, you can rely on your best judgment when picking the right hemline for yourself depending upon the occasion and the time of the day. However, it is best to keep your mini-skirts and mini dresses for after-dark informal occasions. Go for longer hemlines to create a slimmer and taller appearance. A few inches above the knees can also be a flattering length. Use your best judgment to decide what suits you best.

There are also certain unwritten hemline rules that form the cornerstone of elegance:

- To give a balanced appearance, hemlines should ideally always be slightly longer on the back than in the front.

- Pencil skirts and other straight skirt styles should be worn at least one inch longer than fuller styles.

- Full-length coats should be at least one inch longer than all your dresses and skirts.

- Similarly, petticoats, slips and chemises should be at least one inch shorter than your dresses and skirts.

- Pick your heels according to your hemlines. Flats go well with shorter hemlines while heels usually call for longer hemlines.

The way in which your hemline is sewn also speaks volumes about your garment. The ideal hem depth for straight skirts is anywhere between 2 ½ to 3 inches deep. Fabrics that are very stretchy or heavy require narrowed hem depth, ranging anywhere from 1 to 2 inches.

The stitches should always be entirely invisible from the outside. They should be discretely concealed in the thickness of the fabric. If the fabric is very thin, then the hem is stitched to the lining.

In the case of transparent fabrics, the edges are finished through the process of hand-rolling similar to how your handkerchiefs are finished. Delicate material like tulle isn't hemmed at all. Instead, it is just cut neatly in the right proportions.

Coarse fabrics that have a tendency to unravel (like jersey, tweed, knitted wool) should have their edges overstitched before they are hemmed.

Fabric and Cut

The fabric of your outfit matters just as much as its cut. Always choose high-quality fabric in well-cut styles. The neatness of the cut and the quality of the fabric are both crucial for lending the outfit an elegant and sophisticated look.

Opt for natural fabrics as much as you can. Cotton, linen, silk, tweed, pashmina, cashmere and high-quality wool are the essentials of an elegant woman's wardrobe. If you must opt for other fabrics, then choose the semi-natural ones like rayon and modal. You can also go for blends but it would be better to steer clear of something like 100% polyester as it does not breathe well and simply does not feel as good against the skin as natural and blended fabrics do. Even when you do opt for synthetics, make sure that they look and feel natural instead of synthetic.

French women buy fewer clothes but they lean towards buying the best quality ones they can afford. Develop the attitude of long-term thinking – consider how much comfort and confidence each outfit will provide you before buying anything.

Synthetics are uncomfortable and can cause skin irritation. Despite the advancements in technology, it's still difficult to replicate the luxurious feel high-quality natural fabrics provide.

Therefore, before making up your mind about purchasing a garment, read the label (on the inside of the garment where fabric information is embossed) carefully to learn thoroughly about the kind of fabric that has been used to construct it.

You want to not only look good in your clothes but also feel good inside them. Feeling good and looking good are interconnected. When you feel good about what you are wearing, there will always be a spring in your step. Buy fewer clothes but never compromise with quality.

In France, it's perfectly alright to wear the same clothes regularly. Repeating one's outfits doesn't make one look any less elegant. However, adding cheaper quality outfits just to expand one's wardrobe certainly downgrades even the most beautiful woman's appearance.

Chapter 3 - How to Build Your Signature Look

Consistency is at the heart of elegant dressing. Finding your own signature look and sticking to it will not only help you look chic day in and day out but will also remove much of the headache associated with figuring out what to wear.

Therefore, once you have discovered your signature look, you'd want to stick to uniform dressing which means your wardrobe will comprise a limited set of styles, colors and fit that perfectly match your personality and make you look like a million bucks.

When your wardrobe is so carefully planned that every item of clothing serves as a perfect match to your personality, you'll never be standing in front of your closet baffled, "Oh my god, I have nothing to wear." Don't forget to do the closet detox exercise before starting out on your new journey of chic dressing.

Defining Your Staples – Building Your Basic Wardrobe

These pieces will form the base of your signature look so they must be of very high quality and well made. You can mix and match these basic items to create any look – day time to glam night out.

Remember, there are no hard and fast rules attached to building your 'essentials' wardrobe. Follow the tips provided below as suggestions rather than as strict guidelines. It's also crucial to keep in mind your individual personality when building your basic wardrobe. For instance, you might only want to stick to skirts and own more than 2 pairs of them. Perhaps, you prefer wearing trousers or jeans and want to focus on building your wardrobe around them.

Use your judgment to analyze and understand your own personality, then use your best judgment to employ the tips that are best suited to your own individual needs. Now, let's get started:

2 skirts in a classic style (Pencil/A-line or both) – Select one in black and another one in a light color. You can also choose both of them in black and add variety to your wardrobe by selecting different fabric types for both styles. Also, go for a classic length (like the midi style) that will look flattering on all occasions.

2 pairs of pants – Opt for a classic style like cigarette pants or straight fit trousers depending upon what flatters your figure best. I would suggest buying one in black and another one in white. You can also buy both of them in dark colors. Choose a comfortable fabric that also provides a good fit.

2-3 silk blouses – Silk is the most luxurious fabric of all. It instantly upgrades any look without looking over-the-top dressy (provided the cut and style is simple). If you can't afford 2-3 blouses at the moment, then start with just one. Choose it in white or a pastel shade that goes well with the rest of your wardrobe.

2-3 dresses – These should ideally also be in a high-quality fabric. Opt for simple classic designs that will stand the test of time.

2 evening dresses – A beautifully designed silk evening gown is an absolute essential for formal occasions. The best time to buy one is not one day before a special occasion. Instead, buy it when there is a sale at your favorite store. Start out with just one if your budget does not allow purchasing two.

2 jackets – Again, buy one in a dark color and the other one in a light color. Parisian women are very particular about fit. Make sure that your clothes fit you perfectly.

3-4 cardigans/sweaters/sweater dresses – Again, choose from a smaller pool of colors and make sure that the colors and designs complement the rest of your wardrobe.

2 overcoats – The ideal coat should be few inches below the hemline of your dress and skirt. If you can't afford to buy two, then purchase just one in a classic dark color like black. Buy the second one in a light color.

2 pairs of skirt suit/pant suit – One pair should be in a light material like linen. The other pair should be in a heavy material suitable for winter. You don't have to wear the entire ensemble together. You can mix and match the different pieces with other items from your wardrobe.

An assortment of tank tops/t-shirts/camisoles – You can own an assortment of these in different colors. However, I would recommend having black and white as essentials here also. Stay away from T-shirts with graphics on them. They are the exact opposite of chic and certainly don't have any place in an elegant woman's wardrobe. Opt for simple classic designs and go for a well-fitted look here as well.

Again, these are just basic recommendations. A lot of factors will come into play when you get down to planning your ideal wardrobe. You'd want to modify the different recommendations based on important factors like your lifestyle, nature of work, the climate of the place where you live, etc. For instance, a woman who works in the corporate world will need more pairs of skirt suits than a stay-at-home mom. A woman living in a hotter climate will need more summer dresses/skirts than a woman residing in a colder place.

Accessories

Now, this is the fun part. Accessories are essential for adding character and mood to your basic wardrobe. Here's what I recommend:

Scarves/Stoles/Shawls

I highly recommend owning a wide variety of these in different colors and different materials. However, again, I would recommend choosing only the best quality fabrics. You'll own these pieces for a long time and they can add an instant hint of color to any ensemble.

Jewelry/Watch

I truly believe that pearls are an elegant French woman's wardrobe staple. In France, women prefer a minimalist look when it comes to their jewelry – less is more. A high quality real or faux pearl necklace will be your best friend in both formal and casual occasions.

When choosing other pieces of jewelry, go for simple designs that don't scream for attention. Invest in statement pieces that will last the test of time while never going out of style. For instance, your signature necklace can be a white gold diamond necklace with a thin chain and a classic pendant.

I am myself not a huge fan of costume jewelry and I would recommend staying away from them if you aren't already big on them. They can often downgrade a chic ensemble by looking a tad too costumey.

A beautiful watch in gold or silver (or a combination of gold and silver) is certainly one of the best statement pieces you can own. It can instantly upgrade any look. Again, make sure that you pick a classic design and buy a high-quality Swiss watch. If you can't afford it right now, wait until you can. It will last you a lifetime and will be well worth the wait. It is just impossible to replicate the statement a beautiful Swiss watch makes with cheaper pieces that start showing the signs of wear and tear in a few years.

Shoes

With such a wide variety of shoes available in the market, it can be tempting to buy more pairs than a well-dressed woman really needs. Investing in quality is absolutely essential here also.

I would highly recommend choosing only the best quality leather shoes. If you don't already have one, then it's totally worth saving up for it. Skip the pretty looking shoes in lower quality material that come and go out of fashion in no time. Instead, opt for a classic pair of leather shoes in a style that never goes out of style. If you find the idea of purchasing leather opposed to your ethical beliefs, then at least invest in a pair of well-made high-quality shoes that flawlessly imitate the look of leather.

In fact, high-quality leather shoes are an excellent investment considering they age well (provided they are taken care of) and can last a very long time. When you are buying a cheaper pair of shoes, you are not only spending more money in the long run but are also leaving a larger carbon footprint by discarding your old shoes that will likely be added to landfill.

Whatever your personal decision might be in this content, one thing is for sure – quality should dominate quantity when picking your shoes. If you don't have an unlimited budget, then it's best to stay away from trends.

Also, you must invest time and effort in the upkeep of your shoes. Nothing downgrades a look more than an excellent outfit paired with muddy and less than fresh looking shoes. Therefore, keep your shoes clean and polished at all times.

Flats

If you have walked on the streets of Paris, then you already know that flats are the most popular choice with Parisian women for going about their daily activities. Invest in two classic pairs of flats – buy one in a dark color and another one in a light color (suggestions: black and nude). It is best to stay away from white when choosing shoes and bags as they can look quite provincial and are certainly also not easy to maintain. Pick your flats in a classic design that exudes an air of simplicity and minimalism. Your shoes are an accompaniment to your outfit and they should complement the rest of your wardrobe. Therefore, they should never be so eye-catching that they scream for attention. Invest in the darker pair first, and then add the next color as you build up your collection.

Pumps

The best accompaniment to any city outfit is a pair of classic close-toed pumps in high-quality leather. Again, you should have one in a dark color and another one in a light color (black and beige are the best choices). Low to mid heel shoes are much more practical and elegant than high heeled shoes. After all, you can't look elegant when you look uncomfortable and are having difficulty walking. Go for a height that you are comfortable walking in. Open toed shoes are best avoided as they hardly ever look elegant unless they are part of a dressy evening ensemble. Close-toed shoes look classier while also providing added protection to your feet.

Also, I would suggest staying away from shoes with ankle straps. They cut the length of the legs making them appear shorter and stouter.

Dressy Evening Shoes

This is the only place where a truly elegant French woman would opt for open-toed shoes. However, I would still recommend staying away from ankle straps due to the fact that they cut the length of the legs. Instead, brocade or satin high-heeled pumps in a pale or dark color (whichever harmonizes with your evening dresses) can be a much classier style to opt for.

Sports Shoes

Needless to mention, you also need a pair of good quality sports shoes for exercise and other sporty events. Stay away from neon and other over-the-top bright colors. Opt for a dark shade in a muted tone that does not call for attention. It is better to choose dark colored sports shoes since these shoes are most likely to get dirty.

Stockings

The right pair of stockings can make your legs appear flawless. Despite the fact that there are myriads of options available in the market currently, elegant French women prefer sticking to the basics. A neutral beige tone that closely resembles your skin color will be your best bet for light colored outfits. You can opt for sheer black stockings to go with your dark colored outfits.

It is advisable to select the stockings in broad daylight as it can be hard to tell the actual color of a pair of stockings under the bright lights of the departmental store. It is a lot more economical to buy several pairs at once as stockings must be discarded before they start showing major signs of wear and tear. Even the most sophisticated woman can look less elegant wearing a pair of baggy nylons wrinkling around her knees and ankles.

Handbags

Much like the shoes, the right handbag can totally make or break a look. A medium sized handbag is the best choice for daily use. Stay away from large handbags if possible as they don't look elegant at all. I personally prefer structured handbags as they tend to look extremely elegant. I would suggest buying your handbags in high-quality full-grain leather. If you are anti-leather, you can indeed go for faux leather but unfortunately, faux leather doesn't offer the durability that leather provides.

I would suggest owning at least two handbags for daily use. Buy one in tan and another one in black. If you can afford only one, then go for the tan one first since tan can work with any color of outfit including black.

You will also need two clutches for the evening. Again, one in a dark color like black and another one, in a light color.

Chapter 4 - What Not to Wear

We have talked a lot about what to wear. Now, let's take a look at what not to wear.

Shorts

You won't find any French woman wearing shorts on the streets of Paris. The only people you'll ever see in shorts will be the tourists and very young girls. In fact, shorts should not be a part of an elegant woman's wardrobe as they are one of the least flattering outfits out there. Long shorts can be the trickiest to wear. In all seriousness, the boy scout look is far from elegant.

If you have nice legs and are confident about showing some skin, then it's okay to wear very short shorts on the beach or while playing sports. An elegant French woman would definitely not wear them on the streets or while running errands.

Exercise Clothes

Exercise clothes should never be worn except when you are actually exercising. Nothing downplays a woman's loveliness more than keeping herself confined to unflattering exercise clothes all day long. Remember, elegance is all about being appropriately dressed at all times of the day!

Worn Out Clothes

Invest time and effort in the upkeep of your clothes. This way they will last you longer and will show fewer signs of wear and tear. Buying high-quality clothing also automatically means you create less waste and can hold onto your favorite pieces for a long time. However, when your clothes do start showing major signs of wear (gaping holes, fading color, etc.), it is best to discard them. You deserve the best and your clothing should be an extension of the respect with which you treat yourself.

Staying Chic Indoors

A lot of women ignore their appearance when they are in the intimacy of their homes. This really brings forth the question 'who is it all for?' A true Parisian woman would look just as chic in the house as she does outside. She keeps herself looking her best not to put a façade for others to see but as a reflection of the dignity with which she carries herself in both public and in private.

I personally wear the same clothes both indoors and outdoors. Instead of saving my best clothes from getting 'ruined,' I wear them every day. Why should I wait for a special occasion to wear my best clothes? I am special and every day of life is a special occasion.

Before going to bed, I change into my nightwear and dressing gown. On no occasion, would I or any elegant French woman wear worn out t-shirts with holes to bed. It's about loving oneself and not so much about putting our best foot forward for the world to see.

Nightwear

Invest in quality nightwear. We spend a significant amount of time every day just sleeping. Why not allow ourselves the luxury of wearing the most comfortable and luxurious nightwear?

A truly elegant woman would also always keep her robe handy just in case she has to walk around the house at night or in the morning. I would recommend buying 2-3 elegant pair of nighties or night suits for your snooze time.

You'll need two robes – one in wool (for winter) and another one in cotton or silk. It is best to pick a full-length robe in a solid color that will go with all your other nightwear.

Make sure that you keep your nightwear strictly for use at night. Don't just sit around in your pajamas all day long even if you are to stay at home the whole day. How you dress has a significant impact on how you feel about yourself. While dressing down in one's nightwear at night can feel luxurious and soothing, it can make one feel unkempt and lousy if one decides to stay in them all day long.

Dress Up and Stay Dressed

French women stay dressed up even when indoors. Don't save your best clothes for some special occasion. Of course, I am not suggesting that you wear an evening gown at home. But put on your best clothes (that silk blouse you love, the cashmere sweater you are so proud of) when you get dressed in the morning. Don't be too worried about ruining your clothes when doing daily chores. The odds of your clothes getting ruined beyond repair are significantly low. Besides, you can always just don a nice apron while doing chores around the house.

Treat yourself with love and care because that's your true gift to yourself.

Lingerie

What you wear under your clothes matters just as much as what you wear on the outside. The word 'lingerie' itself is French. It was originally derived from the word 'linge' or linen and implied items made out of this delightful fabric. However, in today's times, there is a wide variety to choose from when selecting one's undergarments.

I would suggest sticking to natural fabrics like silk and cotton as they don't irritate the skin the way synthetics do. Wear beautiful lingerie that appeals to you even if no one other than you will see it. It's about how you feel inside because that's what truly matters.

While there are different styles of underwear available, the thong is certainly great for maintaining the shape of your buttocks without any unsightly lines. If you can comfortably wear thongs, then go for it.

When it comes to selecting bras, make sure that they fit your breasts perfectly with no unsightly lumps of flesh peeking out of the corners. It can be even a great idea to take the help of a professional at a good departmental store if you aren't quite sure about your ideal bra size. Wearing the right bra can make a lot of difference to the overall look of any outfit.

Don't save your best lingerie for special days. Wear them every day because you are special and you deserve the best.

Chapter 5 - Hair, Grooming and Make-Up

You can have the best clothes in the most luxurious of fabrics but if you don't maintain yourself well, it will all account for nothing. No matter how generous nature has been to you, after a certain age, you are fully responsible for the way you look.

Hair

Parisian women are known to wear chic low-maintenance hairstyles. Go for a look that suits your face cut. One of the most classic hairstyles in France is certainly the bob. While it looks super chic on many women, it does not suit all face types. Work with your stylist to find a hairstyle that accentuates your features. A sophisticated face-framing shoulder length hairstyle is usually flattering on almost all face types while also being relatively easy to maintain. It is also the most versatile haircut as you can create a wide variety of hairstyles with it.

Keep your hair clean and properly styled at all times. You can leave your hair loose for a day look or try something alluring like the classic French knot. Formal occasions certainly call for an elegant up do.

Grooming

Excellent grooming is absolutely essential for maintaining a chic look. Keep your hands properly manicured and feet pedicured. The condition of a lady's hands have long been considered to be a major giveaway of her social status. You don't need to spend a lot of money getting professional manicures and pedicures. It is very easy to learn to do these yourself in the comfort of your home.

Stay away from tacky nail color and stick to neutral colors or red for painting your nails. Of course, going for the classic French manicure is also an excellent choice. Elegant French women stay away from nail art and other passing trends. Sticking to the basics is the best formula here as well.

Skincare

Establish and stick to a skincare routine. Make sure that you remove all traces of makeup before retiring to bed at night. Pick an AHA based face wash for gently exfoliating your skin on a regular basis. An AHA face wash can safely be used every day. It is also advisable to use a hydrating mask at least once or twice a week. For radiant plumped up skin, you can use a hyaluronic acid based moisturizer.

Makeup

French women use makeup to enhance their best features. Pick a foundation that perfectly matches your skin tone and apply just a hint of blush on your cheeks. Line your eyes with a liner and plump up your lashes with some mascara. French women often use red lipstick for a dramatic effect. You can also create a more natural look by going light on the makeup application. You can also use a light pink or nude lipstick. Makeup should always be all about enhancing your beauty rather than making you look made up.

Exercise and Diet

Staying in top shape is crucial for maintaining an elegant appearance. While it's not common for Parisians to go to the gym, it's quite rare to find overweight people in France. Most of us get our exercise from staying active as walking is the most common mode of transport in this lovely city. I would suggest you find ways to remain active throughout the day.

Make health conscious choices whenever possible – take the stairs instead of the elevator, walk instead of drive as much as you can. If you like the idea of joining a gym or any other kind of fitness classes, then go for it!

Foreigners are often amused by how the French seem to eat everything while staying slim. The secret is portion sizes. Portion sizes are much smaller in France than they are in North America. Also, food is like a sacred art to the French and most French people care about using only the best and finest ingredients in their food. Instead of depriving yourself of your favorite foods, create a more balanced diet. You can learn to cook yourself and then create healthier versions of your favorite items.

Don't forget that the French secret to good health and a great body is 'balance.' Eat in moderation and consume only high-quality food items. Stay away from preservatives, colorants and food additives. Eat freshly cooked meals as much as possible.

Chapter 6 - The Basics of Chic – Inner Values

It won't be misguided to conclude that elegance or chic doesn't just come from the clothes we wear. It is a reflection of our inner values. To appear elegant on the outside, we have to be chic on the inside.

Elegance is an Attitude

Elegance is more than just the way one chooses to dress. It is a way of thinking and a way of life. An elegant woman is a lady of poise and grace. Her style involves an understated glamor which is reflected in her posture and in the way she carries herself. Everything about her reflects the fact that she is confident in her skin. Think about this – you might have seen many women dressed in the exact same way but only one stands out so much. There is something about such a woman – it's more than her outfit and her shoes. She is elegant in the way she sits, in the way she speaks, even in the way she moves her hands. It is, therefore, definitely not just about her clothes although her clothing choices are an extension of her elegant personality.

How to Cultivate Elegance

I truly believe that every woman can transform herself to become a lady of quintessential charm. Below are some tips on how to cultivate elegance in oneself. These tips focus on developing poise and grace which are the cornerstones of elegance. Even the most perfect piece of clothing will not do anything to enhance the personality of its wearer unless the lady possesses grace and poise.

Developing Poise and Grace – The Cornerstones of Elegance

- ➤ Keep yourself looking presentable at all times, even if you are going to spend the whole day at home and no one else will see you. After all, for whom are you doing all this? Your commitment to elegance is your gift to yourself and the only person you truly need to impress is YOU. You must remain committed to who you want to be even if you are going to spend the entire day by yourself. You have truly internalized all the precepts of elegance when you are the same person in both public and in private.

- ➤ Elegant women always have impeccable manners. There's also a certain air of mystery about them as they don't reveal everything about themselves too easily. Focus on developing perfect etiquette as knowing how to act in any situation is a truly empowering thing to have. Since manners are a sort of dying breed in today's day and age, having impeccable manners will truly help you stand out. It will also enhance your confidence levels as you'll start carrying yourself with greater self-assurance.

- ➤ Posture is the most important aspect of an elegant appearance. No matter how expensive an outfit you are wearing, if your shoulders are hunched, it will make you look a lot less attractive. Develop the habit of retaining perfect posture even when you are in the privacy of your home. Great posture exudes an air of self-assurance and a positive sense of pride in oneself. One very useful tip I received at a yoga class is to imagine as if a string is pulling me up from the base of my spine through my head. Try visualizing this to straighten your posture right now. To further develop your posture and etiquette, you can also consider taking posture and etiquette classes. Even if you don't have the time or money to go to an actual class, don't forget that the internet has made it very easy to learn anything and everything. You can learn a lot from simply watching videos and reading articles online. Observe women who have impeccable manners and are eternally stylish. For instance, someone like the Duchess of Cambridge. Thanks to her perfect manners and graceful style, she is a major fashion icon all over the world.

- To be truly graceful, you have to be considerate towards others. After all, etiquette and good manners are all about being accommodative of others and helping them feel comfortable. If you observe any elegant woman, you'd notice that she not only possesses excellent manners but is also thoughtful towards others.

Chapter 7 - Shopping Tips for the Elegant Woman

- Make a list of the essentials you need to buy and stay focused on acquiring them when you go out shopping.

- Note down the names of the brands/shops that best match your style and stick to exploring them. This would save you a lot of time and energy as you'll know exactly where you can find what you need. However, initially, this might require a bit of exploration on your part since you might not already know the brands that best represent your individual style.

- I would highly recommend that you shop alone. Going out with a girlfriend is often a bad idea as envy (even when it is latent) can be a real problem. Despite her best intentions, she might distract you from buying a perfect outfit if she can't afford it herself. Also, shopping alone keeps you more focused on the goals you have set for yourself.

- Find an excellent tailoring shop and get your suits stitched from them as suits look best when they are custom made.

- Always stay on the lookout for deals and sales. They are certainly the best time to buy your favorite outfits. However, don't get tempted to buy a mediocre item that you less than love simply because it is on sale.

- **Buy only those items that you absolutely love. There is no place for mediocrity in an elegant woman's wardrobe.**

- Wear comfortable shoes while shopping – you know you'd be on your toes for a long time!

Wishing you a wonderful and elegant journey to a chicer you!

Conclusion

Thank you again for purchasing this book!

I hope I was able to help you in developing an understanding of living and dressing French Chic.

The next step is to put your newly acquired knowledge into practice. You can keep this book as a handy reference guide for the future. It's always a good idea to reflect on the principles and brush up on the ideas presented in this book every now and then.

Finally, if you enjoyed this book, then I'd like to ask you for a favor. Would you be kind enough to leave a review for this book on Amazon? It'd be greatly appreciated!

Also, don't forget to check out the second book in the French Chic series on Amazon, *French Chic Living: The Ultimate Guide to a Life of Elegance, Beauty and Style.*

Good luck on this journey to a chicer life!

Printed in Great Britain
by Amazon